CORNERMEN

by Oli Forsyth

Cornermen premiered at the Old Red Lion, London, on 30 July 2015.
It was performed at VAULT Festival, London, on 2 March 2016.
The production was restaged on tour on 27 January 2018.

CORNERMEN

by Oli Forsyth

Cast

MICKEY	James Barbour
JOEY	Oli Forsyth
SID	George Jovanovic
DREW	Jesse Rutherford

Creative Team

Producer	Smoke & Oakum Theatre
Associate Producer	Zoe Sofair
Sound Design	Joshua Lucas
Lighting Design	Joshua Lucas
Image	David Lindsay
Trailer Design	David Hall
Website & Brand Management	Emma Forsyth at Little Upstart
Casting Directors	Liam Flemming & Bogdan Silaghi

Special thanks must go to the respective teams at New Diorama Theatre and Red Ladder Theatre for their continued support of Smoke & Oakum Theatre and for making this tour possible. We're also extremely grateful to Julia Tyrrell, Lucy Danser, Anton Melenevski, Stewart Pringle, Ed Harris, VAULT Festival, The Old Red Lion Theatre, The Pleasance Theatre Trust, OtherPlace Brighton, Mark Burford at The Ring Boxing Club and former cast and creatives: Joe Lichtenstein, Andrew Livingstone, Andy McLeod and Adam Bellamy.

BIOGRAPHIES

JAMES BARBOUR | MICKEY
Theatre credits include: *Kings* (New Diorama Theatre); *Till We Meet in England* (Safehouse Peckham), *Epoch 1985* (The Vaults); *Hello/Goodbye* (Vienna's English Theatre); *Cornemen* (Pleasance Courtyard/New Diorama Theatre) and *The Leaving of Things* (Savoy Tup).

TV and film credits include: *Blotter, An Saileach, Magnum Opus, The Pink Triangle.*

Training: East 15 Acting School.

OLI FORSYTH | JOEY/WRITER
Theatre credits include: *Cornermen, Tinderbox, The Cow Play* (Smoke & Oakum Theatre); *Poking the Bear* (Theatre503); *Ashes to Ashes* (Badac Theatre); *Othello, Hayfever* (Dugout Theatre); *Acres* (All The Pigs Theatre); *Hamlet* (Young Shakespeare Company).

TV and film credits include: *Silent Witness, Doctors* (BBC); *My Imaginary Life* (Canister Studio); *Drift* (Madramore).

As a writer, credits include: *Tinderbox* (2014), *Aubade* (2015), *Happy Dave* (2016), *Beast* (2016), *Kings* (2017).

Training: East 15 Acting School.

GEORGE JOVANOVIC | SID SPARKS
Theatre credits include: *Screens* (Theatre503); *Nick* (Broadway Theatre); *Richard III* (Blue Elephant Theatre); *Romeo and Juliet* (Hen & Chickens Theatre); *Market Boy* (The Lost Theatre).

TV and film credits include: *Kiss Me First, Teen Spirit, Doctors, Yoke Farm.*

Training: The Oxford School of Drama

JESSE RUTHERFORD | DREW
Theatre credits include: *Goody* (Pleasance Courtyard/Greenwich Theatre); *Luna Park* (Soho Theatre/ZOO Venues); *Cornermen* (Pleasance Courtyard/New Diorama Theatre); *Chicken Shop* (Park Theatre); *Love In the 21st Century* (Hen & Chickens).

TV credits include: *Halcyon* (ITV); *EastEnders, Doctors* (BBC).

Training: Rose Bruford.

JOSHUA LUCAS | TECHNICAL PRODUCTION MANAGER

Technical credits include: *Almost Always Muddy* (Battersea Arts Centre CTN); *The North! The North!* (Chris Harrisson); *The Raree Man's Peepshow* (Promenade Promotions); *Grandad & The Machine/ Nuketown* (Jack Dean); *Help!* (Viki Browne); *There Shall Be Fireworks* (The Plasticine Men); *Edgar & The Land of the Lost* (Wardrobe Ensemble/The Bike Shed Theatre.)

Venue positions include: Technical Manager (The Bike Shed Theatre); Assistant Technician (Exeter Northcott)

THE COMPANIES

SMOKE & OAKUM
Smoke & Oakum Theatre was founded by artistic director Oli Forsyth as a new-writing company in 2013. Since then they have produced six shows that have gone on in front of thousands of people at venues all over the UK. Of the plays they have created four have been published, the rights to which have been bought by drama schools and companies across the country. Smoke & Oakum shows cover a range of topics, from boxing to rave culture, and always have the same mix of urgency and crackling dialogue that led David Byrne to label them 'One of the best new companies around'.

NEW DIORAMA THEATRE
New Diorama Theatre is a pioneering venue in the heart of London dedicated to providing a home for theatre ensembles, both emerging and established, from across the UK. Since opening in 2010, New Diorama has welcomed well over 120,000 audience members and has developed productions that have toured both nationally and internationally. Having received two prestigious Peter Brook Awards for their programme, New Diorama were also the recipients of the 2013/14 Les Enfants Terribles Prize and Artistic and Executive Director David Byrne was awarded the OffWestEnd Award for Best Artistic Director in 2014.

New Diorama Theatre was also the recipient of the prestigious Peter Brook 'Empty Space' Award in 2016 as a 'vital creative hub for established and emerging theatre companies' and was named Best Fringe Theatre at the 2016 Stage Awards.

RED LADDER
Red Ladder is a radical theatre company with over 45 years of history. The company is acknowledged as one of Britain's leading national touring companies producing new theatre, contributing to social change and global justice. Red Ladder is funded by Arts Council England and by Leeds City Council.

Red Ladder exists to create theatre about and around human struggle. Our work is galvanising and stimulating, generous and life affirming, collaborative and visionary, fearless of and for many people. We help people make sense of the world and understand the power that they and their communities have to change it.

CORNERMEN

Oli Forsyth

For N.E.O.N.

'Now, whoever has the courage and a strong and collected spirit in his breast, let him come forward, lace on the gloves, and put up his hands.'

Virgil

4

Acknowledgements

Special thanks to Charlie Butt, Fenella Dawnay, Julia Tyrrell, Lucy Danser, Ed Harris, David Hall, David Byrne and New Diorama Theatre, Mark Burford and The Ring Boxing Club, Stewart Pringle and Old Red Lion Theatre, The Pleasance Theatre Trust, Otherplace Brighton and the VAULT Festival Team.

O.F.

Cornermen premiered at the Old Red Lion, London, on 30 July 2015. It was first performed at VAULT Festival, London, on 2 March 2016, with the following cast:

MICKEY	James Barbour
DREW	Jesse Rutherford
JOEY	Oli Forsyth
SID	Andrew Livingstone

Director	Joe Lichtenstein
Producer	Oli Forsyth
Lighting and Sound Technician	Adam Bellamy
Video Editor and Image Design	David Hall

Characters

MICKEY
DREW
JOEY
SID

Scene One

*All four actors sit, ready, in a line of four stools behind a
canvas on the floor. The canvas is the stage, whenever an actor
takes to the canvas they are 'on stage', when they exit the
canvas they are, in effect, invisible. The lights focuses in a
square of light onto the canvas as* MICKEY *takes centre stage.*

MICKEY. It's cyclical this boxing game, keeps on turning, that's
    why it's all rounds and rings. The second one lot are done, the
    next generation are starting all over again, heading to the same
    place in the same way. It's because we love it. The only reason
    we know David beat Goliath is because everyone who
    watched kept talking about it. Make two people fight and the
    spectators will come. But no one wants to watch an old fighter.
    We like young blood. So when you've thrown your best shots
    and you don't move as well as you used to, that wheel will
    take you right back to where you started, poor with no
    prospects, and now twenty years older. So every boxer has a
    choice, either they stay on the wheel and hope their time at the
    top gets them enough for the journey back down. Or, they can
    get off, and use that wheel to take them places.

    Transition. MICKEY *returns for his stool as the scene moves
    into 'The Pub' where* MICKEY, DREW *and* JOEY *sit
    searching for ideas. They have been here for some time.*

JOEY. Mark Francis?

DREW. He quit.

JOEY. What about his brother?

DREW. He quit too.

JOEY. Wasn't there a cousin? Swear those boys had a cousin…
    Paddy?

DREW. Peter?

MICKEY. Paul. And he quit at around the same time.

DREW. Besides, none of them were exactly champions, were they?

MICKEY. We're not after champions, are we? We just need someone who can put on a show and sell a few tickets.

JOEY. And stay on his feet.

Beat.

What about Ricky Mayer?

DREW. He's got to be about forty now, we don't want that.

JOEY. Well, at the moment we've got no one so let's not discount him just yet.

DREW. We can do better than a punch-drunk pensioner.

JOEY. Oh, can we? Well, if you've got a young, athletic heavyweight stashed away that wants to sign with us then do point him out, Drew. But until he shows up I say we approach Mayer.

MICKEY. He won't do it. Next fight's his last.

JOEY. How do you know?

MICKEY. I asked him a few months ago. What about Shane Andrews?

DREW. Ah poor bloke.

JOEY. Shane?

DREW. Yep.

JOEY. Why?

DREW. Rick Morris put him to sleep in the second about a year back and he hasn't lasted longer than four rounds since then.

MICKEY. Well, what about Rick Morris?

DREW. He quit.

Collective beat.

JOEY. Christ alive, seven years on the circuit and everyone we knew has quit.

DREW. Or died.

JOEY. Or is shit.

MICKEY. Sam Coulson found God.

JOEY (*shocked*). He didn't.

MICKEY. Yeah. Set up a gym in a prison teaching young guys how to box.

DREW. Can't hold that against him.

MICKEY. Offered me a job couple of years ago... wish I'd taken it right about now.

DREW. Freddie Baker?

JOEY. Quit.

MICKEY. Got knocked out by Poulter last year and packed it in not long after. Good call if you ask me, it was starting to show. How about Saul Burton?

Beat.

DREW. He's not up for it, Mick.

MICKEY. What? He's far too young to pack it in, good fighter too. What's his problem?

DREW. No, he's still boxing it's just... he had some trust issues about us, about the group.

MICKEY. Trust issues?

DREW. Yep.

Beat.

MICKEY. With me?

DREW. Yeah. Well, with all of us really.

JOEY. Oh, terrific.

MICKEY. Why?

DREW. He said there was a suggestion we don't treat our boxers as well as we should.

MICKEY. He really said that? What? Because one fighter gets hurt on our watch suddenly we can't be trusted? I mean, Jesus. We make a couple of bad calls and they turn me into a villain!

JOEY. I know, Mick, it was our names getting smeared as well.

MICKEY. But it's me that prats like Saul Burton want nothing to do with. They don't understand. You have to risk things from time to time in life. I mean this isn't golf, it's boxing for Christ's sake –

DREW. Look, all we need to do is sign someone who wins a few fights and moves up the rankings a bit, then all will be forgotten.

MICKEY. Bloody hope so. Can't work in an industry where no one trusts you.

DREW. Who else? Let's think big.

MICKEY. Hold on, before we carry on with this I could... use a break. Shall we get a drink?

JOEY. Go on then.

MICKEY. Whose round is it?

JOEY. Yours. It's always bloody yours.

MICKEY. All right, all right. (*Beat.*) But let's keep going with this first. We need to find someone.

JOEY. Mike Dennit?

MICKEY. He's thirty-something, Joe. What are we going to do with that?

JOEY. Well, exactly, think about it, he's established. We can book fights using his name and we all get paid. Beats scrabbling around trying to build some kid's reputation.

DREW. And in two years' time we're back at this table in the same situation just with another boxer who everyone saw get knocked about on our watch. We don't want old, we don't want established, we need something new. Something that can grow.

JOEY. Well, help me out, Drew, refresh my memory, how did you get started again?

MICKEY *sniggers*.

DREW. I never got past club level really. I wasn't made for boxing.

JOEY. Shocker.

DREW. Because you were such a star.

JOEY. I went professional.

DREW. For five years. And how many fights did you win?

JOEY. At least I went for it.

DREW. But you ended up in the same place as me.

MICKEY. Which is nowhere.

The confrontation subsides.

DREW. Mick, you did all right when you were younger, how did you get signed?

MICKEY. I got picked up at an amateur night when I was sixteen.

DREW. Well, there we are. Let's get to an amateur night, see what's there.

JOEY. No, no, no. If we go down that road we'll end up with some lanky teenager who still needs toilet training.

DREW. And if we keep going through our phone book we'll end up with some old git who's already got the shakes.

JOEY. Mick?

MICKEY. Well, we're not getting anywhere with people we know. Let's give it a look.

The scene quickly transitions to 'The Amateur Night'.
MICKEY, JOEY *and* DREW *sit facing out to the audience as if watching a fight.*

Scene Two

A bell sounds to start the fight.

DREW. They've had this place redone.

JOEY. They have indeed.

DREW. Used to be a right mess, remember? I don't recognise anyone here.

MICKEY. Well, it's been a while since we last showed an interest in amateurs.

JOEY. Let's not make a habit of it. Right, says here they've got fifteen three-round fights, means we'll see thirty boxers in total, what are we after?

MICKEY. I say middleweight to light-heavyweight.

DREW. Yeah. I can see that. Around the twelve-stone mark.

MICKEY. Not so big he'll be slow but broad enough to pack a punch.

JOEY. Well, these two are featherweights so ignore them.

DREW. We want a worker too. Like Harry Coles, remember? A proper grafter.

JOEY. Okay good, good. Age?

MICKEY. Younger the better.

DREW. But he needs a chin. No good to us if he gets knocked out all the time.

Three bells.

MICKEY. Case in point.

DREW. Saw that one coming a mile off.

JOEY. We could talk to that bloke.

DREW. Nah look at him. Got to be late twenties, we need a bit of youth.

MICKEY. Exactly. It's a fresh start, Joe, we don't want anyone else's bad habits.

DREW. What are these new guys?

JOEY (*checks programme*). Welterweights.

DREW. Little on the light side.

MICKEY. Let's not be picky, if we see someone good we get after them before any of the other managers here do.

DREW. We'll have to be quick.

JOEY. Train them up, turn pro and start booking some fights.

MICKEY. Nice little earner for the next ten years.

DREW. Fifteen if we're lucky.

MICKEY. God, wouldn't that be nice. A journeyman with a good reputation and regular fights.

JOEY. If we could get two or three on the books we'd be –

They all shoot up. Something impressive has just happened in the ring.

MICKEY. Oh!

DREW. Jesus Christ.

JOEY. Big right hand.

DREW. Where did that come from?

JOEY. And again! And again!

MICKEY. Fuck me he's fast!

JOEY. They're going to stop the fight!

MICKEY *springs into action.*

MICKEY. Who is he?

They all look to JOEY.

JOEY. Uh... right, well, says here it's Ferdinand in the ivory trunks and Sparks in the... the noyer?

MICKEY. What the fuck is noyer?

JOEY. I dunno. Ivory is going to be grey, isn't it? Because an elephant is grey.

Beat. They look at the ring.

MICKEY. No one's wearing grey, you tit! I see white shorts and black shorts.

DREW. Black shorts! We want black, that's what noir is.

MICKEY. Right and what's his name?

JOEY. Sid Sparks. Go get him!

MICKEY. Where's he gone?

DREW. The changing rooms.

JOEY. Get going, Mick!

MICKEY. Jesus, fuck, how do I look?

DREW. Fine, fine. Have you got a contract?

MICKEY. Bollocks.

JOEY. Jesus Christ.

MICKEY. All right.

JOEY. One thing you had to remember.

MICKEY. All right!

DREW. Look, just get a bloody handshake. Guilt him into hanging on, we can get him a contract on Monday.

MICKEY. Right, any of you got a tenner?

JOEY. Get out!

MICKEY. It's a good-faith payment. I'll tell him there's more to come. No kid turns their back on money.

JOEY. It's not coming out of my pocket.

DREW *quickly hands over ten pounds*.

MICKEY. Okay, right, Joey, come with me, stand outside and say you're the doctor. Make sure no one else comes in.

They break.

Scene Three

The scene resolves itself into 'The Changing Room'.
DREW/DOCTOR *is giving* SID *the once-over, checking eye movement, looking for any cuts.*

DREW/DOCTOR. And look into the light.

SID *does so*.

Okay, and turn your head left.

MICKEY *enters behind them*.

Any headaches? Pains in the body?

SID *shakes his head*.

Well, looks like you avoided any damage.

MICKEY. Next fight's about to start, doctor, they need you ringside.

DREW/DOCTOR. Right. Right you are. (*Turns to* SID.)

Congratulations, well fought, Sam.

SID. Sid.

Beat.

DREW/DOCTOR. Yes, of course.

DREW *exits, leaving* MICKEY *and* SID.

MICKEY. You want a team that knows your name, Sid.

SID. Who are you?

MICKEY. Mickey Donovan. You ever heard of me?

SID *shakes his head.*

Okay, not to worry. I'm a manager, I run a team of three
other trainers and we all just saw your fight.

SID. Oh yeah?

MICKEY (*hums ascent*). It was a good fight, good stoppage.
Pretty lucky but good nonetheless.

SID. Come off it. It was a great shot.

MICKEY. I'm not saying it wasn't a good punch. I'm just
saying he walked into it.

SID. Why'd he do that?

MICKEY. That's between him and his team.

SID. I think you're talking bollocks.

MICKEY. Well, you're wrong.

Beat.

Are you still in school, Sid?

SID. I'm twenty-one.

MICKEY. Ah. You looked a lot younger out there.

SID. Where were you sat?

MICKEY. Ringside.

SID. I didn't see you.

Beat.

MICKEY. Do you work, Sid?

SID. Apprenticeship.

MICKEY. In what?

SID. Electrical repairs.

MICKEY. I see. Pay well?

SID. It will when they employ me full time.

MICKEY. And when will that be?

SID. A year at most.

MICKEY. You sound very sure, quite cocky for an apprentice.

SID. I'm good with my hands.

MICKEY. I knew that already, Sid.

>*Beat.*

>I've got an idea for you. We were all very impressed with how you boxed out there but you're still a long way off where you need to be if you want to make some money out of this. But we all think that, given the right guidance, you could do very well for yourself, have a back-up in case that illustrious career in repairs doesn't come off. So here's what I'm proposing, come on board with us, we'll get you out of the workshop, train you up and turn you pro.

SID. I need the work.

MICKEY. Once you've turned professional the money comes in.

SID. Only if I win.

MICKEY. Not at all, plenty of journeymen make a good wage.

SID. What so I'll get paid to lose?

MICKEY. No, you'll get paid to fight in front of hundreds of people.

SID. But as filler.

MICKEY (*shrugging*). Lose some of the time, win some of the time.

SID. Lose most of the time.

MICKEY. Or you could spend your life fixing lamps and old ladies' radios. Then you'll be a loser all of the time.

Pause. SID *thinks.*

I'd bet you a fair amount that when that bell went, and the ref lifted up your arm you felt a special little thump right around here, where your ribs meet. (*Points to his solar plexus.*) Like you were the greatest thing that ever lived. I can give you that every day, and I can pay you for it. You've just got to box for me.

Pause.

SID. I need to ask my mum.

MICKEY. Fair enough. And if she says yes?

Beat.

SID. I'll do it.

MICKEY. Good boy. Where are you training?

SID. Riley's Boxing Club.

MICKEY. I know the one. Me and my team will come by on Monday morning to give you a contract and start working. Don't forget, don't be late and don't tell anyone what you're doing until we show up, okay?

SID. Yes.

MICKEY. Good. (*Gives him the ten pounds.*) That's for tonight. Spend some of it on your mum.

Beat.

Shake my hand.

He puts his hand out. SID *takes it,* MICKEY *holds on.*

When boys like you break promises like these it has a way of coming back to haunt them. So don't go running off with any flash gits in suits waving pieces of paper at you, got it?

SID *nods. They shake. The scene very quickly snaps back to 'The Amateur Night' with all three in a line watching the ring.*

DREW. And where's he training?

MICKEY. Riley's in Borough.

DREW. I hate that place.

MICKEY. Well done, Joe. Didn't hear a peep out of anyone else.

JOEY. Wasn't much of a problem in the end.

DREW. Just after you left some kid named Jack Macy put on an
absolute masterclass.

MICKEY. Oh yeah?

DREW. Best I've ever seen. Flattened his bloke in the first
round. Doctor was only thirty seconds late but nearly missed
the whole thing.

JOEY. Look he's only just coming to now, poor kid.

MICKEY. Well, where's this Macy guy then? We could make it
two in a night!

DREW. Doubt that. He's right there with the bigger boys. No
wonder he's smiling.

MICKEY. Oh.

DREW. Yep. No one was that interested in our bloke after
they'd seen that.

DREW *steps forward. Monologue state.*

Scene Four

DREW. We signed Sid Sparks to make us money. That was the
main reason. He was incredibly fast, and the thing with quick
fighters is that they don't get hit so much, means they fight
more, means they make you more money. But the first time
I saw him, I really didn't think that much of him. He was an
investment, and one Mickey was very keen to cash in on. He'd
been talking with this promoter in Brighton who ran a local
club. Anyone who came down and made a fight of it got five
hundred pounds no questions asked. Way we saw it, Sid got
his professional debut, we all got a hundred pounds and if it
went well we could start building Sid's reputation as a
journeyman. Journeymen are the backbone of boxing, most
people only ever hear about the champions and the contenders,
the cream of the crop. But the beating heart of this business
are the guys you never heard of who fight any opponent and
expect to lose. If a journeyman gets a good reputation he can
make a nice living out of losing, build a career. But at that
point Sid had no reputation, no history and therefore no say
over who he was fighting. Which is a very dangerous thing.
So only three weeks after signing him, we all went down to
Brighton for Sid Sparks' professional debut.

Scene Five

MICKEY, DREW *and* JOEY *snap into a line looking diagonally across the ring at an imaginary boxer of epic proportion.* SID *warms up behind them, out of earshot. The mood is one of fear and tension.*

JOEY. Jesus Christ.

DREW. Oh bollocks.

MICKEY. I know.

DREW. No way on earth is that man a welterweight.

JOEY. He's massive.

MICKEY. I know.

JOEY. He's gonna kill him.

MICKEY. Shut up, Joe.

JOEY. Well, he is. Look at the fucking size of him!

DREW. He's gotta be six two.

JOEY. Did you know this was who he'd be fighting?

MICKEY. Did I know he'd be fighting the Incredible bloody Hulk? No, Joe, they failed to mention that.

JOEY. Oh my God.

DREW. This is not good, Mick.

MICKEY. I know.

DREW. I mean this is not a smart move.

JOEY. It's his debut for Christ's sake.

MICKEY. Right, all of you shut up. No more talk about Sid getting hurt, he doesn't need to hear it.

JOEY. We should pull the fight, Mick, we should let him back out.

MICKEY. And how do we get paid if he doesn't fight? If he doesn't go in there we leave with nothing so stop crying and start getting him ready. No one will expect him to last long so if he can make a fight of the first few rounds we'll still get that five hundred. Okay? Bring him in.

MICKEY *and* DREW *turn to collect* SID. JOEY *becomes the* REF, *who walks to the front of the stage to deliver instructions to the boxers. All four actors look up to give the idea of the size of the opponent.*

JOEY/REF (*with great relish*). All right. I want a clean fight. Nothing below the belt, no heads and no elbows. When I say break I want a good break. In the event of a knockdown the aggressor must go to a neutral corner and I will start the count of ten. Obey my commands and protect yourself at all times. Touch gloves and come out fighting.

They go to break.

DREW. How you feeling, kid?

SID *nods. Massaging. He begins to bounce and limber up. Shadow-boxing.*

MICKEY. All right, Sid. Time for you to dance. Stay off him for a while. Lead with the left for the first few and keep moving. We can start poking at him when you've found your range.

SID *nods.*

Come here. (*Grabbing him closer.*) There's no shame in going down a little easy. No one wants to see you get hurt.

MICKEY *inserts the gumshield.* SID *turns back, stands, and begins to focus across the stage at his opponent.*

JOEY. Let's be busy, Sid.

DREW. Stay on your toes, watch him tire.

MICKEY. Pop, pop, pop just like we practised, yeah?

The bell rings. SID *trots out into 'The Ring' offstage, controlled and confident.* (*Note, at no point do we see* SID *actually fighting.*)

They watch. DREW *steps forward.*

DREW. That night Sid threw two hundred and fifty punches
landing an incredible hundred and thirty-five. He didn't put a
foot wrong all night. And we watched, absolutely
dumbfounded as this kid came to life under the lights. Before
he'd been some kid with quick hands but now... now he was
different. Suddenly we realised there was more to Sid than just
a journeyman, we'd been sat on a gold mine and not seen it.

Beat.

After that first fight we stayed in the south of England for
about a year, fighting regularly and winning, so by the time
we returned to London he was already more successful than
any boxer we'd managed before. He was a name, which was
great for the fights, but it meant he became part of a world
that we knew nothing about. Cameras and contracts to fight
guys high up in the rankings. And we didn't know how to
handle it. On the one hand we wanted to enjoy the success,
the glitz and all that, but on the other we could see it was
getting to Sid. To go from nothing to a name in eighteen
months threw him, and it threw some of us. Mickey though,
he didn't blink, he was constantly at every other boxer
around. If they were higher than Sid in the rankings he'd do
everything he could to make them fight, so the bouts got
harder and harder. After one year in London Sid Sparks was
ranked as the twelfth best welterweight in the UK and set to
fight Mark Hayward, one of the biggest names of the last
generation. And we were just about holding on to him.

Scene Six

The scene changes to 'The Press Conference'. MICKEY, JOEY and SID sit in a line. JOEY and MICKEY are covering all the questions that SID fails to answer and loving the attention.

DREW/REPORTER. Sid! Next week you fight Mark Hayward to solidify your place as a top-ten British boxer, nervous?

Beat. SID doesn't answer.

JOEY. Of course we're not. Sid Sparks is the next generation of British boxing and we're ready to show that.

MICKEY (*painfully pensively*). Yeah, and I think what my colleague is trying to say is that it's all about hard work so we've got no reason to be nervous.

DREW/REPORTER. Is that right, Sid? You're not concerned about the gulf in experience?

Beat.

MICKEY. You see experience, we see age. Thirty-eight is not young.

DREW/REPORTER. So you think you can do it? Beat one of the most decorated boxers in British history?

JOEY. Absolutely.

MICKEY. No question.

DREW/REPORTER. Sid?

Beat.

SID. Yeah, I can.

DREW/REPORTER. Okay. (*Moving on.*) Now obviously the big talking point in British boxing at the moment is the rise of new welterwight wonderboy Jack Macy who recently claimed the British title in emphatic fashion. Did you see the fight, Sid?

SID. No.

DREW/REPORTER. But you heard about it?

SID *looks around for support, then:*

SID. I heard it was quite a knockout.

JOEY. We're not here to talk about Jack Macy –

MICKEY. Other fights with other boxers are none of our
    business.

DREW/REPORTER. But they will be if you win next week.
    If you beat Hayward you'll have to go on to face the likes of
    Hooper and Kosky and Macy who are certainly not thirty-
    eight and who are, at the moment, a class above.

    Beat.

SID. I take each fight as it comes, I don't want to speculate on –

MICKEY. Sid Sparks is the best welterweight in Britain. When
    we're done with Hayward we'll continue to challenge up the
    rankings. If any other boxer thinks they're good enough to
    beat him you tell us where to sign.

    They break.

Scene Seven

The scene resolves itself back to 'The Pub'.

MICKEY. He just sat there!

JOEY. Yeah.

MICKEY. Just sitting – not saying anything.

JOEY. Yeah.

MICKEY. It's an interview for christsakes, he had to say
    something.

JOEY. You'd have thought.

MICKEY. But no, all this 'I take each fight as it comes.' How
    about selling some bloody tickets?!

JOEY. I hear you, Mick.

MICKEY *sits*.

MICKEY. I worked months to get this fight and he can't even talk it up.

Pause.

DREW. Howard had a point.

JOEY. Eh?

DREW. He had a point. If Sid beats Hayward we're going to have to think seriously about who he fights up the rankings.

JOEY. Slow down, Drew. They'd eat him alive.

DREW. My thoughts exactly but he disagrees, what was it, Mickey? 'The best welterweight in Britain'?

MICKEY. What's wrong with that?

DREW. Asides from the fact it's not true?

MICKEY. Ah, shut up.

DREW. He's not even close.

MICKEY. I was trying to shift tickets.

JOEY. Never know, might rattle Hayward.

DREW. Don't be silly, Joe.

JOEY. What?

DREW. Mark Hayward is the most experienced boxer in the weight class. He's not going to get rattled by some kid and his team mouthing off on TV.

JOEY. Maybe now he's getting older…?

DREW. No chance. He may be getting on but I watched him fight Lanyard at Wembley last year. Tough as old boots that man.

JOEY. Can't be that confident. I heard he's trying to dodge Jack Macy.

DREW. Everyone's trying to dodge Jack Macy.

MICKEY. And what was that about Jeff Beck? Since when has Sid been hanging out with pop stars?

JOEY. No idea. I've noticed the hangovers though.

MICKEY. He was a mess yesterday.

DREW. We don't exactly set a great example, having our meetings in here.

JOEY. What's wrong with The Albion?

DREW. Nothing, nothing. Maybe he's just blowing off steam. He's only twenty-four after all.

MICKEY. He should be focusing on the fight. That's his job. Joey, have a word, will you? Try and settle him down, it's getting silly.

JOEY. Yeah, will do. Shall we head back?

MICKEY. Yeah, course. How's he looking?

JOEY. Good as ever.

MICKEY. Is he planting his front leg on the jabs?

JOEY. He's jabbing like he jabs, Mick, since when was his leg a problem?

DREW. Where's his head?

JOEY. Not like he's ever had an issue with nerves.

MICKEY. Maybe not, but mark my words, second Mark Hayward steps into that ring and starts moving about he'll be shitting himself. C'mon let's go.

They walk downstage to the very bottom then turn, in a line, upstage. MICKEY, JOEY *and* DREW *face towards the audience. They are preparing themselves, doing hair, checking pockets, etc.*

Scene Eight

DREW. Joe, might not hurt to pack some extra cottons.

JOEY. Yep.

MICKEY. I've got some already.

JOEY. Can't hurt to be prepared. Don't want him to get cut and then run out of gear.

Slight pause.

MICKEY. Might want to pack some extra Vass as well then.

JOEY. I got it, Mick.

Pause.

MICKEY. How we doing, Sid?

Beat.

Sid?

SID *appears. He looks tense, ready to fight.*

JOEY. Here he is.

DREW. Feeling okay?

SID *nods and sets himself, he's already begun twitching.*

JOEY *starts working his neck and shoulders (note: this is done in the way an owner pets a dog, it's unconscious for both parties). Gloves on.*

SID. You're all looking very dapper.

MICKEY. Well, someone's got to take the attention off you.

SID. No chance of that.

JOEY. That's it. Good boy.

Pause. MICKEY *has either procured some pads or goes bare-handed. He holds up his hands and calls out the punch he wants which* SID *responds with. They constantly move and bounce throughout this exchange.*

MICKEY. One.

SID *instantly responds with a left jab.*

Good. One.

Punch.

Good. On your toes. Come in, one-one, and then out.

SID *starts to bounce, takes a step in, throws two jabs, and bobs just out of reach.*

Again.

Repeat.

JOEY. Stay off him.

MICKEY. Good. One, two, roll and six.

SID *jabs a left, a right cross,* MICKEY *drags his left hand over,* SID *rolls under to throw a right to the ribs/*MICKEY'*s right hand.*

Again.

Repeat.

And then a one-two.

SID *throws a one-two.*

Good.

There is a momentary pause when MICKEY *is still stood in range and* SID *has just finished throwing. He relaxes a tiny bit before throwing a five-five-three-two with incredible speed and aggression. None of these make contact, it's simply a burning-off of adrenalin.*

JOEY. Attaboy.

More rubbing, massaging from all. They slowly group around SID *so he is facing the audience, hands on him like a group of bodyguards.*

DREW. Ready?

SID *nods. They move forward.*

DREW/ANNOUNCER. Ladies and gentlemen, in the red corner weighing in at a hundred and forty-three pounds... Sid Sparks!

They huddle upstage-left as if by a turnbuckle.

JOEY *steps forward.*

JOEY. Mark Hayward had been around for years. He was an immovable part of boxing, like the furniture. We were all terrified of what would happen if Sid got caught or lost concentration for a few seconds. Hayward could have knocked him out with either hand and in big fights like that one it helps to have been around a bit. But we were in the same boat as Sid, we'd never been that far or fought someone that good. We just had to hope the work we did paid off. But we had a plan. We knew Sid wasn't going to knock Hayward out, he was hardly a power-puncher, so that fight was going to be decided on points or it was going to get stopped. The longer the fight went the more chance there was of Hayward catching Sid so we focused everything into getting the fight stopped. We had to give the referee a good enough reason to call it off. Now an old-timer like Hayward, he's got one of those faces. Scar tissue on scar tissue, all around the eyes. This big craggy brow like elephant's skin. That was our ticket. Flesh that's been knocked about over the years is easier to split open. And, as he's a right-handed boxer, he'd have taken most of these shots to his left side. So we sent Sid out for that fight with one very clear instruction.

MICKEY (*back in the corner*). Go get that eye.

Mid-round, all are shouting advice. These should be somewhat coordinated, not just mindless shouting, have a build, moment of doubt, moment of success.

Careful now. Stay off him, stay off!

JOEY. Right! Right, keep your eyes on the right.

DREW. Dance, Sid, side to side! Christ.

JOEY. Wrap him up for fuck's sake, Sid.

MICKEY (*to* DREW). He can't take many more of those.

DREW. Stay off the fucking ropes, Sid, Jesus!

JOEY. Hook's coming, Sid, hook's coming!

Slightest pause as they watch the punch get thrown. Sudden elation.

Good boy! Cut and move.

MICKEY. Double it up, pop pop.

DREW/ANNOUNCER. Ten seconds!!

JOEY. That's it, Sid, keep at him with those jabs!

DREW. Follow him in! Let's be busy!

JOEY. Now with the right, no fucking daylight!

DREW. Yes!

MICKEY. Jesus! Attaboy!

Bell goes. All swarm forward as SID *appears on the stool. Vaseline goes on, water bottles, No Swells, massage, cold coins to ears, etc., etc. Like a pit stop, incredibly efficient and coordinated. The other two work while* MICKEY *talks to* SID.

SID. He hits like a hammer.

DREW. Breathe it in.

SID. He doesn't bloody stop!

MICKEY. Good boy. Good boy. That's it breathe it in. Deep breaths. Now listen, he's running on fumes at the moment, he's got very little left. Keep making him swing and miss, he won't like it. And his left comes down after throwing it, you see that? Just for a second, a little wobble. Means he's getting tired. So every time he throws a left, you're straight in there with the counter, see how that works for a few rounds.

JOEY. Busy, let's be busy.

MICKEY. And keep at that eye! It's starting to really swell up, you see that?

SID *nods*.

Keep poking away at it. He can't last long, soon enough his hands are going to drop and when they do you go straight in with the right, y'hear? Pop it open like a fucking blister.

DREW. Breathe.

MICKEY. I want his eye cut so large you lose your glove in it.

SID *nods*.

DREW/ANNOUNCER. Ten seconds!

MICKEY. Right, on your feet, show him how fit you are.

DREW. Keep dancing about.

JOEY. And stay away from his big shots. He caught you a few times back there.

MICKEY (*placing his hands on* SID's *face*). Stick to the plan, this is yours for the taking. Go get that eye.

SID *nods. Bell.* SID *moves out, the others stay at the turnbuckle.* JOEY *moves forward.*

JOEY. Thing about cuts is they bleed. Obviously. They become big red markers that a boxer is hurt which everyone can see. Now mouths, noses, ears, they all bleed, hit them enough times and they'll start to show it but eyes… eyes are the worst. They gush blood, they're almost impossible to stem, and it's the cut most likely to get a fight stopped. See, to a referee, a boxer with big swollen eyes that won't stop bleeding can't see what's going on, can't defend himself and therefore shouldn't be allowed to continue. Fight gets stopped. For eight rounds Sid had done nothing but jab at Hayward's left eye and the swelling was growing out of his face like a poppy. We had to just wait, either Sid would get caught, or he'd split Hayward open.

Back to the corner.

MICKEY. Good boy!!

DREW. Double it up.

MICKEY. Oh!

JOEY. Now get out, now get out!

MICKEY. Smooth as you like, look at that!

DREW. Don't get cornered.

JOEY. Watch the feet, the feet!

DREW. God, he moves well.

MICKEY. Keep at him, no breathing room!

JOEY leaps forward.

JOEY. For two more rounds this went on. Hayward swinging
wildly, Sid slipping out of the way where he could and
always, always poking at that left eye. Until eventually
Hayward walked straight into a right cross and –

ALL (*as* JOEY *lands the imaginary punch*). Boom.

JOEY. Such a pretty river of red like nothing you've ever seen.
Ten rounds of swelling and damage all goes pouring down his
chest, onto his shorts and dripping down onto this immaculate
white canvas. Perfection. Sid kept hammering away and soon
you could see these big red marks where Sid was leading him
around the ring. Looked more like bullfighting than boxing.
On and on around that ring he went until, in the eleventh
round, Sid Sparks established himself as a genuine contender,
someone to be reckoned with. We were going to have to fight
the bigger boys now, whether Sid was up to it or not.

Bell, all group together.

ALL. Ladies and gentlemen, your winner by way of technical
knockout… Siiiiiiid Spaaaaaaarks!

All four actors raise their arms in celebration with SID *in
the middle, they savour the moment then slowly transition
into:*

Scene Nine

All actors are on stage getting ready, they check their appearance in imaginary mirrors behind which sit the audience. MICKEY, DREW and JOEY are all tense and fussing in the mirrors. SID is calm and collected.

JOEY. How do I look?

DREW. How do I look?

JOEY. You look fine.

DREW. You too.

MICKEY. I'm sweating.

JOEY. So am I.

DREW. Why are we sweating?

JOEY. We're nervous.

MICKEY. It's our party, why are we nervous?

DREW. It's not our party.

JOEY. It's a party for us.

MICKEY. Right, but why am I nervous if the party's for me?

SID. The party's for me.

Beat.

DREW. Eh?

SID. The party's for me. It's to celebrate my victory.

Collective 'ooooh'.

What? I won the fight. I get the party.

MICKEY. And who got you that fight?

JOEY. And who got you ready?

MICKEY. Exactly.

DREW. We're a team, Sid. No one got here on their own.

MICKEY. So whose party is it, Sid?

SID. It's our party.

ALL. Exactly.

Car horn.

JOEY. Taxi's here!

ALL. Bollocks!

The tempo increases.

JOEY. Do I smell all right?

MICKEY. There's a stain on my shirt.

DREW. Don't rub it!

MICKEY. What do I do?

DREW. Just leave it.

JOEY. No one will notice.

DREW. They'll be looking at your face.

SID. They'll be looking at me.

JOEY. Shut up!

SID. There's no stains on my shirt.

MICKEY. Do you want one?

DREW. My hair won't stay down.

JOEY. My hair won't stay up.

MICKEY. Am I balding?!

Beat. All the boys look in the mirror to MICKEY.

DREW. No chance.

JOEY. Course not.

DREW. Just a tight cut.

JOEY. It's all the rage.

SID. We're gonna be late.

ALL. Shit!

JOEY. Ready?

DREW. Ready.

MICKEY. Ready?

SID. Born ready.

> *They all change places and are at the party. They line up at the bar. 'Let's Dance' by David Bowie builds on the speakers.*

MICKEY. This is amazing.

JOEY. Look at that dance floor.

DREW. Look at that bar.

SID. Were all these people at the fight?

MICKEY. Guess so.

SID. Wow.

JOEY. Always looks smaller from under the lights.

DREW. Four pints please.

MICKEY. Go easy, Sid.

SID. It's my night off.

JOEY. Go easy!

SID. You lot are no fun.

DREW. Come on. Let's grip and grin.

ALL. Cheers!

> *They move. Music grows.*

MICKEY. Hi.

JOEY. How you doing?

DREW. All right?

SID. I'm Sid.

JOEY. Enjoy the fight?

DREW. Oh isn't he just?

SID. I wasn't worried. You know from the first punch.

JOEY. Never doubted him.

DREW. Oh he's a great boxer, great kid too.

SID. Bled all over me!

MICKEY. Onwards and upwards now.

JOEY. No, thank you for coming.

DREW. What did you say your name was?

MICKEY. I like your dress.

SID. Come on let's get a drink.

JOEY. I love to dance.

MICKEY. So where are you from then?

DREW. Can I get your number?

SID. Sorry I've got a girlfriend.

ALL. Sid's got a girlfriend?

SID. But how about that drink?

ALL. Go easy!

DREW. Fancy a dance?

JOEY. Try to keep up.

They dance into each other and reform as the four.

MICKEY. This is the best night of my life!

JOEY. My head's spinning.

DREW. Not bad for a small investment, eh?! Have you ever been anywhere like this?!

MICKEY. I could kiss him.

SID. Please don't!

DREW. Aw, he's embarrassed.

JOEY. Pissed too, I reckon.

MICKEY. He's right, Sid. We don't want to be working tonight. This is about us. We deserve it. All those years of working with rubbish fighters.

JOEY. In terrible venues.

DREW. For no money.

MICKEY. Exactly. This is our night, so drink it in.

ALL. Cheers!

MICKEY. Let's dance, boys!

They strut out to the other end of the dance floor and begin to move. The music builds and builds reaching a fever pitch before lights out. Short.

Scene Ten

Lights up on SID *skipping with a hungover* JOEY *watching him. The skipping goes on for some time before:*

JOEY. Question for you, Sid. When did you get a girlfriend?

No answer.

You been keeping little secrets from me?

SID. Go away, Joe.

JOEY. What? I'm just asking, trying to imagine what the life of a top-ten boxer is like.

SID. Well, you should have tried harder when you were younger.

JOEY. Those who can't... So when did Heather creep onto the scene?

SID. I was seeing her before I signed with you lot, now piss off.

JOEY. Is that how you charmed her? Being an unsociable little gobshite?

No answer.

No, I know what it is. I know why she fell for Mr Sid Sparks. It's all that skipping. Tell me I'm wrong. Tell me she didn't go crazy for a bit of skipping.

SID. Shut up, Joe.

JOEY. No no, I think I'm on to something here.

JOEY rises and goes to stand beside SID. *He mimics skipping. Testing it out. This is very off-putting.* SID *snaps and stops.*

SID. Fuck off, Joe, I'm working here.

JOEY. Well now, that's no way to talk to your team. Bit sore today, are we? I thought you looked a little worse for wear the other night.

SID. Something to say, Joe?

JOEY. No no, nothing. Just I thought a fit young lad like yourself might handle his hangovers a bit better.

SID. How would you know how I handle my hangovers?

JOEY. Well, this might come as a shock to you, boyo, but I've had to watch you train like this quite a few times.

SID. Spit it out, Joe.

JOEY. You like a drink. That's all I'm saying. No shame in that.

Beat.

Go on.

Stand-off over, SID *resumes skipping.*

Probably something your old man liked as well. Dunno, I've never met him but these things do tend to flow downhill.

Pause.

My old man liked a flutter. Y'know? Not too bad either, he often picked a winner.

Slight pause.

But you know what they say, a little knowledge can be a dangerous thing. Bigger the bet, bigger the loss. But that's the trouble, isn't it? Cos if you like it, and I mean really like it, then the loss never seems as bad as the chance of winning seems good.

Slight pause.

I stay away from bookies. I always figured that if something ate your old man, and he tasted good, chances are you'll probably taste all right as well... y'know what I mean, Sid?

No answer.

You know what I mean.

Pause.

Was your dad a dancer too? Cos I reckon the shapes you were cutting last night must've evolved over generations –

SID *stops skipping.*

SID. Jesus, Joey! Shut up!

JOEY. All right, all right!

SID. I'm just saying /

JOEY. I know, I'm sorry /

SID. I'm just saying, I'm trying to fucking work here and you're going through my family tree.

JOEY. I know, you're right. Sorry. All I'm saying is... the boozing hasn't gone unnoticed, and you might want to think about... I don't know, staying in every now and then.

SID *doesn't respond.*

I reckon that's time, old boy.

SID *drops the rope, moves, bobs. Stretches out.* JOEY *notices him stretching and decides to test his reflexes. Throws a one and a one-one that* SID *dodges.*

SID. Not bad for a hangover.

> JOEY *resumes and throws a one-two, one-two – one-two-three –* SID *doges all and catches him in the ribs on the last combo.*

I should train like this more often.

JOEY. Five years ago I'd have had you.

SID. Does that make you feel better?

> *Enter* DREW.

DREW. Sid, masseuse is here.

SID. All right.

JOEY. Lucky boy. What I wouldn't give for a nice rub-down every time I worked up a sweat.

SID. Piss off. They really hurt.

JOEY. My heart bleeds for you.

> SID *goes to leave.*

SID. He's been trying to hit me, Drew.

DREW. Tragic. How late were you last night?

SID. Yeah, yeah.

> SID *exits.*

DREW. I'm amazed he was in today. State he was in the other night.

JOEY. I've had a word.

DREW. And?

JOEY. And what? He listened. He's twenty-four, likes a drink, there's only so much I can say.

DREW. It's not the drinking itself, it's the way he acts when he's had a few. Right little shit. You might need to try again. Did you see him?

JOEY. Didn't need to, I could smell it on him this morning.

Enter MICKEY.

MICKEY. Good morning, all you pretty things.

JOEY. All right, Mick?

DREW. All right?

MICKEY. I am indeed all right. One might say I'm positively giddy.

JOEY. And why's that?

MICKEY *holds up a brown paper file.*

DREW. What's that then?

MICKEY. I've just come from the offices of KingPin Promotions.

JOEY. Yeah?!

MICKEY. Oh yes.

DREW. And?

MICKEY. In three months' time we fight the number-three welterweight in the country, Gary Hooper.

JOEY. You're joking.

MICKEY. Joey, look deep into my eyes and see that I shit you not.

DREW. How'd you get that?

MICKEY. I've been trying to book us a bout with the bigger boys since Hayward. Hooper was keen.

JOEY. Ducking Macy by any chance?

MICKEY. I would imagine that had something to do with it. But his loss, our gain. We decamp to Manchester in two months' time.

DREW. Manchester?

MICKEY. Yeah.

DREW. Why are we fighting in Manchester?

MICKEY. Hooper's from Manchester. He's the bigger name, he chooses where we fight.

DREW. We'll be fighting in Hooper's backyard.

JOEY. Sid's got fans.

DREW. Sure, but they're not going to travel to Manchester for a non-title fight, are they?

MICKEY. It's more than that, Drew. This fight decides who gets to challenge Macy for the title. Or that's how they're going to sell it.

Beat.

DREW. What?

MICKEY. Chances are Macy will fight the winner –

DREW. You're angling for a fight with Macy?

MICKEY. Yes, Drew, of course I am. Why wouldn't I?

DREW. Macy would kill him.

MICKEY. Maybe. Maybe not.

DREW. It took Sid eleven rounds to beat a granddad.

Beat.

MICKEY. They're paying for our gym, our house, our travel, our wages while we're up there and a cut of the tickets win or lose. For that much I'd have Sid fight anyone.

DREW. And what if Sid's not up to it and takes a beating?

MICKEY (*elated*). We still get paid.

Beat. DREW*'s not convinced.*

What's the point of having a boxer at this level if we don't cash in?

JOEY. Exactly.

MICKEY. Good. I want him on every radio channel and chat show there is.

DREW. Sure we want him out so much?

MICKEY. What d'you mean?

DREW. Well, you know how he is. We don't want to make things a bit more… puritan?

MICKEY. Joey's going to have a word.

JOEY. Already had one.

MICKEY. Problem solved. Get him ready, chaps, we leave in two months. Oh, Sidney?! We need your autograph.

Scene Eleven

They break. The scene resolves itself into 'The Train', two seats facing two seats. MICKEY and DREW are already seated. The scene begins with the sounds of a station and JOEY escorting a delicate SID into the cabin and onto his seat.

DREW. Here he bloody is. I was starting to get worried.

MICKEY. What time d'you call this? Train's about to leave.

JOEY. Some of us had to collect Sleeping Beauty.

They conduct this following exchange in full knowledge that SID is there, like angry parents.

MICKEY. Oh, I see. What hour was it this time, Joe?

JOEY. Him and his lady-love were pushing four o'clock.

DREW. Is that so?

MICKEY. Drew, weren't we rising at a similar hour to pack up some ungrateful sod's gym?

DREW. Yeah, that rings a bell.

MICKEY. And I'm guessing that when this wayward child did return home he was a picture of responsibility and sobriety?

JOEY. I'm sorry to disappoint you but he could barely kick off his shoes.

MICKEY. That, Joey, is heartbreaking. Good night was it, sunshine?

Beat.

SID. Yeah... I met Springsteen.

Beat.

DREW. Bruce Springsteen?

SID (*yawning*). Yeah. We went to one of his gigs with Heather and we got invited backstage so I went along. It was good.

Beat.

DREW. Did he do 'Born in the USA'?

SID. Yeah.

Beat.

JOEY. What about 'Dancing in the Dark'?

DREW. Oh yeah.

Beat.

MICKEY. Well... well, you can kiss goodbye to that sort of thing for the next month, we've got work to do.

JOEY. And you better get down to it. No more pissing around with pop stars.

Slight pause.

DREW. Right, I could use a stretch.

He rises.

Cup of tea, anyone?

JOEY. You're all right.

MICKEY. Give him a hand, Joe.

Beat.

JOEY. Okay.

They leave.

Pause.

MICKEY. Springsteen, I ask you.

SID *shrugs.*

You all right?

SID *nods.*

Beat.

You should be chuffed. Hooper was guaranteed to fight Macy before you showed up. You must be making waves.

Beat.

SID. Did you see Hooper's last fight? Against Keller.

MICKEY. Yeah.

SID. He's fast.

MICKEY. That he is.

SID. Reckon he's faster than me?

Beat.

MICKEY. Quite possibly.

SID. Why couldn't I fight down the rankings? Hayward was a tough fight.

MICKEY. You fight up, not down. We want to win titles so we fight the best.

SID. Easy for you to say.

MICKEY. You don't want to win titles?

Beat.

SID. Why do we have to rush? Can't I enjoy this for a bit?

MICKEY. You're not paid to enjoy it. You're paid to win the fights I book you.

SID. And what if I lose?

Beat.

MICKEY. I'm sorry?

Beat.

SID. I don't want to be embarrassed.

MICKEY. No, you just want to waste your time by going out every night.

SID. Here we go.

MICKEY. You have got to sort this out, boy. We're aiming at a title here, this is as big as it gets.

SID. Yeah, yeah.

MICKEY. And this time it's not an old man. You think Hayward was hard just wait until you see Hooper box.

SID. I have seen him.

MICKEY. So why are you pissing around like this? I'm trying to build you a career.

SID. Oh fuck off, Mick.

MICKEY. Excuse me?

SID. You're building me a career? As if you were riding first class before I showed up?

MICKEY. Oh, what are you on about?

SID. You're sorted because of me, Mick. All of you are. And when I'm done my name will be your ticket to get the best guys in the next generation and get rich off them too. After this you're set, next forty years or so you're set. I'm done in ten and then I'm right back where I started. What else am I gonna do? Be a doctor? (*Beat.*) I can count the years I've got left on both hands. So excuse me if I enjoy them while they're here.

MICKEY. You sound like a child.

Beat. SID *leaves.*

They break. DREW *steps forward.*

Scene Twelve

DREW. Looking back now, that fight tastes the worst. An event that big would be the high point of most people's careers but… we just weren't ready. We lost Sid in Manchester. Nothing worked, pleading, shouting we even followed him a few times but we just couldn't convince him that all his pissing around might catch up to him. Trying to explain the idea of losing to a guy who hadn't lost yet was… hard. We didn't seem able to do it. And it just felt odd to me. This was a big stadium fight, the stuff of dreams, and we just let it get the best of us. Of Sid. I mean one day we're working in some damp gym with a leaking ceiling, and the next thing you know we're dropped into a state-of-the-art facility, camera crews outside and Sid's face on twenty-foot posters all over the city. But instead of getting on with the job we just fought amongst ourselves.

We are instantly in 'The Gym'. SID *is doing pads with* JOEY *while the others watch.* SID *has done something wrong.*

MICKEY. No, no, no, no!

SID. What? What fucking now? Eh?

DREW. Same as before, Sid.

SID. What you're starting now as well?

DREW. Well, if you were listening we wouldn't be having this bloody problem, would we?

SID. What?

MICKEY. How many times, Sid? You go in after that left to the body and he's going to clock you time and time again.

SID. Thirteen professional fights, I never once got caught like that. Stellar, Michaels, Hayward, not once, not ever.

MICKEY. But this isn't someone you can dance around. I'm telling you, we've watched the fights, you go in like that against Hooper he's going to take your head off.

JOEY. He's not lying, Sid. He'll put you to sleep every time.

SID *softens a bit.*

SID. But, Joe, if anybody can go in and out without getting caught it's me. You know that.

JOEY. Not against Hooper, Sid. He's lightning fast.

SID. What, faster than me?

Beat.

JOEY. Yeah.

DREW. He's right.

Slight pause.

SID. How can you be this negative? You're all supposed to lift me up.

MICKEY. And you're supposed to show up on time –

SID. Do me a favour, Mick –

MICKEY. On time and ready. You were late again this morning.

SID. Barely.

MICKEY. Half an hour late, and another half-hour to get ready. It's not on.

SID. Well, what's the point of me showing up if all I hear from you lot is that I'm not doing it right and I'm going to get a smack? What's the point?

He makes to leave.

JOEY. Sid mate, come on.

MICKEY. We're not done here, Sid.

SID. We are for today. I'm the one who has to go out there so I'll say when we're done. If that left is going to get me hit then you geniuses put your heads together and find a way for me to get at his body without being knocked out.

SID storms off.

MICKEY. What an idiot.

DREW. Yeah.

MICKEY. I mean honestly, what are we doing here messing around with that?

JOEY. He'll get there eventually.

DREW. It'll be too late, Joe, he'll get what we're on about after the first few rounds but by then he won't be able to do anything about it.

MICKEY. Unbelievable. Closest I'll ever get to a title and that prick ruins it.

Beat.

JOEY. So what do we do?

DREW *steps forward.*

DREW. By the time we walked out, Sid was barely talking to us. We were stood in the tunnel, ready to go and Mick asked Sid how he was feeling. Didn't even answer, just walked out into the crowd like he was untouchable. Supreme confidence. But the thing about boxing, is that it keeps you honest. If you don't take it seriously, take your opponents seriously, it'll show. And if you've been out every night and fighting with your team. You'll stand out like a sore thumb.

Cut to the corner. All shout encouragement.

MICKEY. Move your head, Sid!

DREW. Back off.

JOEY. That's it, hold him off.

MICKEY. No, no, no.

JOEY. Not to the bloody ropes, Sid.

DREW. Oh Jesus.

JOEY. Wrap him up for christsakes, wrap him up.

DREW. Good boy.

MICKEY. Now, nice and easy, pick your spots.

JOEY. Oh for fuck's sake!

Big reaction.

DREW. It's the third time he's gone to the body.

MICKEY. He's out of ideas.

JOEY. Thirty seconds left, Sid, just stay off him.

DREW. What is he doing? Get off the bloody ropes.

JOEY. Side to side, Sid!

DREW. Cover up!

MICKEY. Oh Jesus.

JOEY. Watch the right.

Big reaction.

DREW. Shit, he's cut.

MICKEY. Where?

JOEY. Just under the right eye.

MICKEY. Oh no.

JOEY. He's out on his feet.

DREW. Hang on, Sid!

MICKEY. Make sure everything's ready. I want that cut sorted by the next round.

JOEY. Got it.

Bell goes. They surge forwards. SID *slumps into the stool, totally spent.*

MICKEY. Water, Drew.

JOEY. How bad's the cut?

DREW. Not great.

JOEY. How're the ribs?

SID *is puffing so hard he can barely speak.*

DREW. Check his eyes.

> MICKEY *clicks around* SID*'s face. He responds but not enough.* MICKEY *claps in his face.*

MICKEY. All right, switch on, Sid.

SID. He's so fast.

DREW. Easy, easy, deep breaths.

JOEY. Think his nose is starting to bleed.

> JOEY *is rubbing his ribs or applying cottons to the nose,* DREW *attempts to cool the right eye.*

MICKEY. Sid, you have got to stop going in after his body. He's caught you four times now.

SID. I can't get near him. I can't slow him down.

MICKEY. Well, start picking off his head. He can't move quick if he's dizzy.

SID. He'll have me.

JOEY. And stop going to the bloody ropes. Move about a bit, don't make life easy for him.

MICKEY. Exactly. What happened to dancing about, in and out?

SID. I stand off him he just closes me down.

MICKEY. Stay out of the corners and use your left to keep him away. He can't stay fast forever.

SID. And what if that doesn't work?

> JOEY *doubles around the team and becomes the referee.*

JOEY/REF. How's that cut?

MICKEY. Yeah he's fine, ref. No problems here.

JOEY/REF. He needs to start protecting himself.

MICKEY. He's fine.

JOEY/REF. If I don't see a change in the next round I am stopping this fight.

MICKEY (*turning to face him*). Why don't you just keep your eyes on the fight and I'll see to my guy, all right?

JOEY/REF *leaves the stage*.

DREW. What's he banging on about?

MICKEY. Says if he doesn't see a change he's going to stop the fight.

The action stops.

JOEY *returns and moves towards the audience*.

JOEY. There are lots of ways to get ahead in a fight and if you've been around a bit you'll know most of them. It can be something as simple as gearing up the crowd, or something a bit nastier like breaking up the padding in the gloves. This is the murkier side of boxing. If your fighter is in trouble and doesn't have any answers you need to find a way to give him the edge. The way we saw it, we hadn't come all this way to have our chances ruined by Sid not doing his work. It was up to us. We had to get him an edge.

Back to action. In amongst the flurry of activity MICKEY *is thinking*.

DREW/ANNOUNCER. Ten seconds!

MICKEY. Drew?

DREW *looks up*.

What d'you reckon?

Beat.

DREW. Yeah.

MICKEY. I mean, he's going to stop the fight.

DREW. Yeah.

MICKEY. Joey?

Beat.

JOEY *nods*.

Drew, give me the juice.

DREW *ducks into his bag*.

JOEY *comes forward*.

JOEY. Nowadays Monsel's solution is banned. But we used to use it to stop cuts leaking. Slows down the rate of bleeding, see. But you had to be very careful when putting it on because, if it got in the eyes, it was incredibly painful. Now, if someone says 'juicing the gloves' what they mean is that you put something on your boxer's gloves that will irritate their opponent's eyes. This could be a type of oil or a salve, or possibly Monsel's solution, if you've got it to hand. Sid was already cut so we were going to use it anyway, Mick just rubbed a little bit on Sid's gloves. All he had to do was land a few punches on Hooper's forehead in the next round and hey presto, Hopper's eyes started streaming. Should've taken about two rounds to wash out. Sid only needed one and a half. No one checked. Why would they? You don't expect it at that level and once Sid started landing good shots it looked like any other knockout. And what were they going to accuse us of? Treating our fighter's cut? It could easily have been a mistake.

Beat.

It wasn't. But it could have been.

Bell rings. Lights. In the dark we hear:

DREW/ANNOUNCER. Ladies and gentlemen! Your winner, coming by way of knockout, Siiiiid Spaaaaarks!

They break and transition into:

Scene Thirteen

We're in 'The Massage Room'. It's been a few days since the fight. DREW *is examining* SID, *trying to work out the toll of such a tough fight. He asks him to move body parts, arms, etc., and works on any stiffness.*

DREW. Right arm.

> SID *rolls his right shoulder in his socket.*

> Stiff?

SID. On the back.

> DREW *begins to massage him.*

DREW. Enjoy your weekend off?

> SID *nods.*

> Good. Good. Nice to see Heather?

> SID *nods.*

> So what did you do? Left arm.

SID. Don't really know. Sort of just sat in my room.

DREW. Ah, that's not good.

SID. I know.

DREW. Whole point of a weekend off is that you use it to... I don't know, do something a bit more normal.

SID. Yeah.

DREW. Besides, you just got your first professional knockout. You're usually ecstatic after a win.

SID. Didn't feel like a win.

DREW. I see.

> *Beat.*

SID. You know that glove thing?

> DREW *pauses.*

> Didn't Ali do something like that to Liston?

DREW. Other way around but yeah.

SID. You ever done it before?

Beat.

DREW. Not personally, no.

Beat.

SID. And Mick?

DREW. I doubt it. It was pretty extreme, Sid.

SID. But you'd all talked about it?

DREW. You didn't give us much of a choice.

Pause.

SID. So what happens now? Career-wise, where are we going to now?

DREW. Oh. Well. We've been trying to whip up a bit of a storm while you've been recuperating. Trying to call Macy out and get a title shot for you. Obviously the fight didn't go too well but you finished it like a pro and Macy just wiped the floor with Clarke so –

SID. I listened to it. Sounded brutal.

DREW. It was something to see, but the point is he'll be looking for opposition. After Joey took you back to the hotel we all went out after the cameras and tried to talk it up. Mick said Macy was a coward if he didn't fight you, I thought it was a bit strong but, lo and behold, this morning Mickey gets a call from his management 'regarding a potential fight'.

SID. Really?

DREW. He's over there right now as a matter of fact.

SID. So I'm going to fight Macy?

DREW. Possibly. For a title, Sid.

Pause.

Well, don't look too excited.

Beat.

SID. Joe said most boxers are dodging Macy. Fighting down.

DREW. Well, maybe. Makes it easier for us.

SID. I saw Macy fight the night I beat Hayward.

DREW. After you won? I thought you were with the doctor?

SID. I snuck out.

DREW. Right.

SID. And I watched him, from the tunnel.

Beat.

DREW. Okay.

SID. It was the night he beat Narakov.

DREW. I remember. What are you telling me for?

Beat.

SID. Hooper was dodging Macy, right?

DREW. I don't know.

SID. He was number three in the country, could have fought Macy for the title whenever he wanted. But instead he chooses to fight me, to fight down.

DREW. Well, you insulted him on TV.

SID. What, so he risks a shot at the title to settle a grudge match with me?

DREW. I'm not sure on the intricacies of his plan but –

SID. Drew. He fought me because he knew he couldn't beat Macy. So if Hooper couldn't beat Macy and I couldn't beat –

DREW *clocks what* SID *is getting at and stands in front of him. The tone is no longer one of support or sympathy.* DREW *is angry.*

DREW. Shut up.

Silence.

If you had worked harder, you would have beaten him on your own without us.

SID. Drew –

DREW. If you had worked harder, you would have beaten him on your own without us.

SID. I shouldn't be at this level –

DREW. If you had worked harder, you would have beaten him on your own without us. Say it.

Beat.

SID. If I had worked harder, I could have –

DREW. Don't fuck around with me, Sid! You would have – 'I would have'.

SID. If I had worked harder, I would have beaten him on my own without you.

DREW. That's right. You have got to sort this out – (*Points to his head.*) This is what ruins fighters. This. If you start doubting, and feeling sorry for yourself, then you can fuck off back home right now.

SID. Got it.

DREW *is apoplectic.*

DREW. You are Sid Sparks. And you will take any boxer, and I mean any boxer Mick puts in front of you, I don't care how big, or how tough he is, and you're going to get him in front of you and you're going to hit him, and you're going to hit him, and you're going to hit him, until he is unconscious, on the canvas, with a broken jaw and bleeding from both ears, you understand me?

SID *nods.*

Stand up.

SID *stands.*

When these go – (*Slaps arms.*) and when these go – (*Slaps legs.*) you will have nothing left but the scalps you took and the money you got for cutting them off. How much have you got, Sid?

SID. Some.

DREW. Do you think 'some' is enough? For all the years you've got after? For Heather? For your kids? Do you think that'll pay for the house and the car and the suits and the hospital bills?

SID. No.

DREW. Me neither. So, what are you going to do?

SID. I'm going to work.

DREW. That's right. We're going to work. And then what?

SID. I'm going to win.

Beat.

DREW. Good boy. (*Pulls him in and strokes/ruffles* SID *the way you would a dog who's just had a scare.*) Good boy. Good boy. You know we're always watching out for you.

Enter MICKEY *and* JOEY *who see* DREW *and* SID. *They cross and begin to massage and flick punches at* SID.

JOEY. He's back!

MICKEY. Looking pretty as ever I see. How're you feeling?

SID. Bit stiff.

MICKEY. Well, you earned it. What did you do with your weekend then, Sid? Piss away all your winnings?

SID. No.

DREW. Sat in his room apparently.

Beat.

MICKEY. Well, I'll be. Maybe Hooper managed to knock our message into you. I must remember to thank him.

SID. Fuck off, Mick.

MICKEY. All right.

Pause. MICKEY *smiles at* SID.

How much do you love me, Sidney?

Beat.

SID. What?

MICKEY. Would you say your love for me is a family love?

SID. Sure, Mick.

MICKEY. So in the same way I love you as a son, you would say you love me as a father.

SID. Why not?

MICKEY. Father Christmas perhaps?

Beat.

SID. Well, that depends, Mickey, have you brought me a present?

MICKEY (*with a look of mock surprise*). It's funny you should ask that, Sid. (*Brandishes a brown folder.*) In six months' time you fight Jack Macy, at Wembley Stadium. For the British welterweight title.

Beat.

SID. How much?

MICKEY. We need to hash out the details. This is just an agreement for the match-up. Still need to agree on the number of rounds, referee, glove weight and that.

SID. But roughly?

MICKEY. A lot.

Beat. SID *looks at* DREW.

You'll need a pen, Sid.

Scene Fourteen

They break. The scene is now 'Backstage' at a talk show. SID *is sat down as* MICKEY *and* DREW *run through the information. Mirrors surround the room. Over the Tannoy we hear 'Sid Sparks to make-up please, Sid Sparks to make-up.'*

MICKEY. Be polite. Be charming. Be funny and sell the fight. Yes?

SID. Yes.

MICKEY. Good. Off you go.

JOEY. Oh, and tell them to go easy on the make-up, don't want a repeat of last time.

SID. Yeah, yeah.

JOEY. You looked like a satsuma.

SID. Piss off!

  SID *exits through the door.*

JOEY. He's a real charmer that one.

  Beat. They look around.

  I could get used to this.

MICKEY. Well, give it year or two, sign a few more fighters, maybe win a few belts. We could be here permanently.

  Beat.

DREW. When are you meeting the Macy team?

MICKEY. Tomorrow. You should come along, could use another head in the negotiations.

JOEY. What's left to arrange?

MICKEY. Sticking points really. Glove types, weight and all that.

JOEY. They'll want to make life difficult.

MICKEY. I know. We just have to hope they go along with it.

DREW. And what if they don't?

MICKEY. Then I'm guessing the gloves get heavier and the fight weight goes up.

DREW. To what?

MICKEY. I don't know.

Beat.

JOEY. So what we're saying is that the chances are Sid goes into this fight against a much heavier opponent with added weight on both hands.

DREW. That's not good enough.

MICKEY. It might have to be.

DREW. He'll get nailed.

MICKEY. Look, if we kick up a fuss about any of these conditions they'll just threaten to pull the fight. Macy has already got the belt, it's not like he needs to fight us.

DREW. Well, if that's how they're going to act we should let them cancel it.

JOEY. What?

DREW. If talks break down over a technicality then neither side loses face, Sid keeps his reputation and we buy ourselves another year before we start thinking about Macy again. That'd be a blessing.

JOEY. You don't think he's going to win?

DREW. Come on, Joe. After watching the Hooper fight do you really think he's going to win? Sid doesn't.

MICKEY. Why are you being so pessimistic? He's undefeated.

DREW. Had a bit of help with that though, didn't he?

JOEY. Jesus, shut up. There's people all over the place.

Beat.

MICKEY. You want me to try and get the fight cancelled?

DREW. Possibly, yeah.

MICKEY. Why?

Beat.

DREW. Because he's going to lose, Mick. As sure as sunrise, he'll finish that bout on the flat of his back. And then it'll be over for him.

JOEY. Always a rematch.

DREW. And change what, Joe? I've watched every bout Macy has had since the night we got Sid and he's better than him. He's just a better boxer. So was Hooper, and we can't pull that trick again.

MICKEY. Come on.

DREW. I'm telling you, Mick, we put Sid up against Macy and he loses, we're not back here next week. We'll have to start all over again.

MICKEY. So we start again.

DREW. Just like that? You're forgetting how we got here, Mick. Starting again means another Hayward, another Hooper, not to mention all the fights before he gets back to that level. Hayward was an old man and he got lucky with Hooper, I don't think we get that lucky again. Sid shouldn't be at this level, he said it himself. If he falls out of the spotlight now he'll have to drag himself back into contention with his fucking fingernails. And even if he does, and he comes back, and he gets another shot at Macy, he'll get beaten. They're just better.

Beat.

If we call it off we could buy ourselves at least another year at the top.

JOEY. And leave Macy alone?

DREW. Yeah. I think so.

MICKEY. Turn down a shot at the title? You're mad.

DREW. Surely it's better than him losing.

JOEY. They've all got to lose eventually.

MICKEY. Exactly. And if it's not against Macy it'll happen two years down the line when he's really falling apart. He'll get humiliated in some knackered town hall in Birmingham rather than at Wembley with fifty thousand people watching.

DREW. Better for him though.

MICKEY. Do you know how big the ticket cut is on a championship fight?

Beat.

DREW. No, Mick. I don't.

MICKEY. It's large.

DREW. You're not the one who has to earn it.

MICKEY. Jesus Christ. I can't believe this. He's a boxer, Drew, a prizefighter. That's his job. Our job is to find the opponents and get him paid.

DREW. But your concern isn't Sid getting paid. It's about you, Mick. It's about your pockets.

MICKEY. Well, I'm sorry if that seems callous to you but I don't intend on living the rest of my life in a rented flat above The Albion.

DREW. Neither do I, but if we handle this wrong that is exactly the life we're going to give Sid. When his legs are gone and his brains are scrambled and we've squeezed every last penny we can get out of him then that's the life we'll be giving him.

JOEY. He's not an idiot, Drew, he knew what he was getting in to when he went pro.

DREW. Come on, Jim. He wouldn't know his arse from his elbow if we weren't around.

Beat.

MICKEY. I think he can win.

JOEY. So do I.

MICKEY. And if not then that's the life he chose. I'm not missing my chance to win a title.

The Tannoy cuts through with: 'Sid Sparks to the stage please, Sid Sparks to the stage'.

JOEY. Come on, that's us. Let's watch him sweat.

Scene Fifteen

They break. We are now watching 'The Talk Show'. Canned applause. DREW/ALEC *is introducing* SID *and* JOEY/TYLER, *they enter one after the other shaking hands and doing the casual talk before an interview.* JOEY/TYLER *is a grotesque parody of smooth Hollywood types.*

DREW/ALEC. Hello, hello, hello and welcome back to *The Late Show* where tonight we're talking to a very special guest. The man chosen to wrest the title from Jack Macy's hands, the one, the only, Sid Sparks! And next to him actor Tyler Brantree! Now, Sid. You're ranked fourth in the welterweight division yes?

SID. Number four yes, shortly to be number one.

DREW/ALEC. And still undefeated?

SID. Last I checked.

JOEY/TYLER. Whoa.

SID. Since returning to London I've had fourteen fights, won them all.

DREW/ALEC. Now I think most people would be happy with being number four in that weight class and having a nice undefeated record, but it isn't quite enough for you, is it? So on July 25th you'll be fighting Jack Macy for the British. Welterweight. Title. Is that correct?

JOEY/TYLER. Jesus, man, is that right?

SID. That's absolutely right, yes. July 25th at Wembley Arena I'll be taking the title from Jack Macy.

JOEY/TYLER. Oh my God.

DREW/ALEC. So you think you've got him?

SID (*laughing slightly*). Well, I mean, I wouldn't have taken the fight if I didn't think I could win it.

DREW/ALEC. Can we go on the record and call that a prediction? You're going to win this fight. Care to pick a round.

JOEY/TYLER *and* DREW/ALEC *laugh at this absurd suggestion.* SID *leans out of his chair to look at* JOEY/TYLER.

SID. Tyler, want to pick a round?

JOEY/TYLER *is amazed.*

JOEY/TYLER. Oh my God! Oh my God!

DREW/ALEC. You've got to be joking! You're going to let him pick the round you're going to win in?

SID. Why not? It'll make things interesting.

JOEY/TYLER. That is super-confident, man.

DREW/ALEC. God, this is amazing. So, Tyler, go on, tell us, which round do you want Sid to finish Macy?

Beat.

JOEY/TYLER. I dunnoooooo man, I just – I dunnooooo. It's a big thing to ask, y'know?

DREW/ALEC. You seem overwhelmed by the pressure here, Tyler.

JOEY/TYLER (*looking up*). I mean I just caaan't get over this guy's spirit. He's just got so much truth in him, y'know? And I feel like... round eight?

DREW/ALEC. Eight?

SID. Eight it is.

JOEY/TYLER. Oh my God.

DREW/ALEC. You heard it here first.

SID. Macy betting be watching so he's knows when to book a
taxi for.

JOEY/TYLER. Holy hell, man. Boom! You totally got him.

DREW/ALEC. On that note we're going to head to quick break,
don't go anywhere, when we come back Sid here is going to
give Tyler some boxing lessons for his upcoming film
Jailbird 2: The Man Who Flew the Coop, don't go away.

They break. JOEY *and* SID *wait for the arrival of* MICKEY
and DREW *in 'The Gym', perhaps putting on gloves and
pads, ready for work.*

Scene Sixteen

JOEY. He didn't.

SID. He did.

JOEY. What, he just came out with it after the show?

SID. The cameras were still running. Band was playing us all
out and he just leant over and asked me to do it.

JOEY. Star in his movie?

SID. Not star in it, think he wanted me to play a butler or
something.

JOEY. Well, I hope you told him you were busy.

SID. I did.

JOEY. In no uncertain terms.

SID. Absolutely.

Beat.

JOEY. Star in a movie. Honestly.

SID. Act in a movie.

Beat.

JOEY. No one ever asked me to star in a movie.

SID. Well, I'm shocked, Joe, I really am. Hollywood's poorer for it.

JOEY. Ah shut up.

SID. Temper, temper.

MICKEY *and* DREW *enter.*

JOEY. All right? How did it go?

DREW. Not great. Mickey rolled over like a bloody dog.

MICKEY. I did not roll over.

JOEY. Define 'not great'.

SID. I'll go get changed.

DREW. No, no, stay here. You need to hear this. They got everything they wanted.

MICKEY. Drew –

JOEY. Gloves?

Beat.

MICKEY. Twelve ounces.

Beat.

SID. Okay.

JOEY. Fight weight?

MICKEY. Top weight allowed is a hundred and fifty pounds.

Silence.

JOEY. He fights at a hundred and forty-three pounds, Mick.

MICKEY. I do know that, Joe.

JOEY. A hundred and forty-three. Means when he steps up to fight Macy he's going to be seven pounds lighter than him.

SID. And my gloves will weigh four ounces more than usual. Did you get me anything?

MICKEY. Asides from thousands of pounds?

SID. Oh sorry, I didn't realise money is going to stop him tearing me apart. Did we get anything that will help me in the fight?

MICKEY. Fifteen rounds.

Beat.

They wanted twelve rounds, we got fifteen.

JOEY. Oh, well, nothing to worry about then. Storm in a teacup.

MICKEY. Shut up, Joey.

Silence.

It's been two years since Macy had a fight that went past eight rounds. That's two years of early showers and not running the miles. You think he'll be ready for fifteen rounds? No. So you're going to give it to him.

JOEY. Fifteen rounds won't mean a thing if Macy catches him in the fifth round and knocks him out, like he knocks everyone out.

SID. Exactly.

MICKEY. Well, then we don't let him, do we? He wants an eight-round brawl? We don't let him have it.

JOEY. So the plan, as it stands, is don't get hit by him?

MICKEY. Yeah. We work on your feet and your fitness, make it impossible for him to catch you. The full fifteen, that's the plan. Watch him get more pissed off and more puffed up trying to close you down and then bam! Before he's seen it coming we win it on points. We box clever. If he wants your unbeaten record he'll have to wrench it from you.

Scene Seventeen

DREW. And action in five, four, three…

They break. Throughout this scene, SID cuts between commercials and exercises. They should flow seamlessly into each other. The first commercial is for shampoo.

SID. Hi, I'm Sid Sparks. In boxing you've always got to keep a clear head. That's why I use Head and Shoulders 2in1 shampoo. The combination of cool mint and soothing Aloe Vera –

DREW. Time!

SID is skipping and the team watch, giving him encouragement, this carries on for around ten seconds.

JOEY. And action in five, four, three…

SID. Hi, I'm Sid Sparks. People often ask me how I stay in such great shape and my answers always the same. Drink British milk. Nothing helps your body like the natural –

DREW. Time!

MICKEY and JOEY drag a skipping rope across the stage at head height which SID bounces under throwing ones and twos as he surfaces.

MICKEY. And action!

SID. Hi, I'm Sid Sparks.

Throughout this exchange DREW/CHILD helps SID put on his gloves like an enthusiastic assistant.

DREW/CHILD. Gee, Mr Sparks, you always look so calm in the ring. How do you do that?

SID (*forced laugh*). Well, Timmy, that's simple. I stay calm because I know that if anything happened to me PLO Life Insurance will ensure my loved ones are taken care of. (*Ruffles* DREW*'s hair.*) PLO, always keep your guard up.

On this final phrase he puts his hands up which, when JOEY *calls 'Time' stay in place as he does pads with* MICKEY *pushing him backwards, cutting, slipping and landing lots. Throughout,* MICKEY *continues to call out combinations.*

DREW. Good. Time.

They all clap and encourage SID.

Looked good, light, fast.

MICKEY. Ready for some running?

SID *nods*.

JOEY. Course is he, look at him. Jack who, eh? Jack fucking who?

MICKEY. That's right, won't lay a paw on you. Come on, more to do.

DREW *steps forward*.

DREW. He'd never looked so good. Totally together, no messing around or going out, he was up every morning to run, work in the day and after training he'd go back to Heather. Perfect. Just like when we signed him.

Beat.

The others seemed to take it all in their stride, maybe they were focusing on the fight, but it really threw me. I couldn't get past the fact that we had signed Sid to be a journeyman, a no one, a boxer who gets paid to lose and be forgotten. And then there I was getting phone calls from new up-and-comers and walking into the dressing room at Wembley arena. And it was all because of him, because of Sid. Guess I should have thanked him.

Scene Eighteen

Back to 'The Dressing Room'. JOEY, MICKEY *and* DREW *are getting ready, packing bags, adjusting jackets.*

MICKEY. How we doing, Sid?

> *Beat.*

> Sid?

> SID *appears.*

JOEY. Here he is.

DREW. Good lad.

MICKEY. Looking good.

> *They start working on him. Warming up his hands, etc.* SID *begins to bounce.*

> Ready?

> SID *nods. They face each other.* MICKEY *throws two elaborate and complex combinations that* SID *slips, cuts, blocks and evades, finishing each one with a strong counter.*

DREW. Good.

JOEY. Be busy. Good.

SID. Feels good.

MICKEY. Course it does. You're ready, Sid, you're ready for this.

> *Lots of encouragement, massage, etc.* MICKEY *pulls* SID *closer.*

> When that bell goes at the end of round fifteen, where are you going to be?

SID. On my feet throwing punches.

JOEY. That's right.

> MICKEY *draws* SID *closer.*

MICKEY. Bring me that title okay?

SID *nods.*

DREW. Ready?

They all put their hands on SID*'s shoulders for the ring walk as before.*

DREW/ANNOUNCER. Ladies and gentlemen, the challenger, weighing in at a hundred and forty-three pounds, with a record of fourteen wins and no defeats... Sid Sparks!

We snap to the turnbuckle, tense, ready.

Ten seconds!

JOEY. Switch on.

MICKEY. Right. This is it, Sid, time to go to work. What's the plan?

SID. No knockout.

MICKEY. That's right. Slip, slide, move about, if he catches you with anything wrap him up, go straight in with the clinch, get out, set yourself, and go back to jabbing, got it?

SID *nods.*

Don't let me down, okay?

Bell. Out. JOEY *steps forward.*

JOEY. It was very nearly all over in the first round. We should have seen it coming really. These guys had been building up for months, waiting, chomping at the bit, and then suddenly here we are with a massive crowd, and someone says 'go'. Macy came out like a shot, straight at Sid throwing these enormous punches, head, body, hooks, crosses, everything he had. I remember watching him chase Sid around the ring, throwing these knockout shots, you could feel the air coming off them, and Sid's backpeddling away trying to soak them up.

Bell. DREW *steps forward,* JOEY *steps back.*

DREW. We set him straight and got him ready for the next round assuming it would be the same but from the second round on the fight changed. Macy relaxed, backed off, starting really boxing, not brawling. After the intensity of the first round we were all a bit shocked, and so was Sid, he kept waiting for a barrage to come at him but it didn't. Macy just circled around, picked his spots and started jabbing away. No one expected him to fight like that. It was terrifying.

Cut to turnbuckle.

JOEY. That's right one-two. Keep at him.

DREW. Good boy.

JOEY. Stay off him now, go easy.

DREW. Back up, back up!

MICKEY. Why isn't Macy chasing him in?

DREW. He must be banking on a long fight as well.

JOEY. Guess he didn't fancy chasing Sid around if he couldn't knock him out.

MICKEY. Out the corner, out! Out!

JOEY. Good boy.

MICKEY. What so he's just going to go easy all night until he sees an opening?

JOEY. Looks like it.

MICKEY. Well, that fucks our plan right up.

JOEY. What do we do?

DREW/ANNOUNCER. Ten seconds!

MICKEY. If he's changing his plan, we should change ours.

JOEY. To what?

MICKEY. I'm thinking.

DREW. Think quick. Bell's about to go.

JOEY. That's it, Sid. Double them up!

Bell goes. SID *sits, they swarm around him.*

SID. What's he fucking doing?

DREW. Easy, easy.

SID. He's not supposed to fight clever.

MICKEY. We just need to shock him is all, make him revert to his usual way of fighting.

SID. Well, I'm all ears.

MICKEY. Go at him. In this round, go for him. He's not expecting you to come forward, it'll piss him off and he'll start swinging again.

JOEY. Yeah, throw a few more, let go with the punches.

MICKEY. No, don't just throw more. I'm saying the next time you land a jab, Sid, don't back off out of range after. I want you to follow it in with lefts to the body and come upstairs with your right. Scare him, rough him up, he won't like it.

DREW. Up, up, up.

MICKEY. On your feet, Sid. Go get him all right?

DREW *steps forward.*

DREW. It was a bit unorthodox I'll admit, but Mick had a point. Macy and his team had completely sussed us out. All the negotiations about glove size and weight class meant we had put all our focus into making sure the fight went the distance. But when Macy showed up also ready to go the full fifteen we had to try something new or it was home time. We had to rile Macy, upset him, we figured that if Sid could embarrass him, or make him look bad then Macy would revert to fighting in his usual style and we could get on with our game plan. No champion wants to sit back and soak up punches. So at the start of round four we sent Sid out to get him.

Back to the corner.

MICKEY. Come on, Jack! Make a fight of it!

JOEY. Pick your spots, Sid!

DREW. What are you waiting for? An invite?

JOEY. Don't back off, let him come at you.

MICKEY. Come on, Sid, come on.

DREW. Wait for it, find your mark.

MICKEY. Any second now.

JOEY. Wait for him to come to you.

DREW. Here it comes.

JOEY. We'd been waiting for it all round and then suddenly
Macy moved forward and flicked out a jab at Sid's head. He
slipped it perfectly, leaving Macy just off-balance and then…
(*Makes the motion of a left jab as the others sound it out.*)

ALL. Boom!

JOEY. Sid throws out this left.

ALL. Boom!

JOEY. He lands another and then…

ALL. Crack!

JOEY. He lands a right straight onto Macy's nose. More out of
surprise than anything Macy stops moving forward. There
was a split-second pause, and then Sid went at him.

Back to corner.

MICKEY. That's it! That's it!

DREW. No fucking daylight!

JOEY. Keep at him!

DREW. Right! Now with the right!

JOEY. Follow him in!

MICKEY. Stay with him, Sid!

JOEY. Jesus Christ!

DREW *comes forward.*

DREW. The entire atmosphere changed in a second. All the spectators sat in total shock as they watched the champion, Jack Macy, backpedalling away from our Sid, hunched over, trying to hold back an avalanche. Sid drove him halfway across the ring with his punches, left, right, head, body, fast as he could. But you can't throw all that without something coming back. When Macy hit the ropes he let them take all his weight, leaning way out and then cannoned back in, slipped Sid's left and threw the biggest counter he could. It was this enormous right hook, massive, I saw it starting in his feet and twist up his body like a spring. A wild, desperate punch but lethal and right at Sid's head. I watched this huge haymaker, screaming towards his head, Sid, still surging forwards, Macy flying off the ropes and then, with inches left, Sid rolled, not perfectly mind, but he did enough. The weight of Macy's punch carried on, dragging him around, so by the time Sid came back up Macy was off-balance and unguarded. He was just there, head up and ready for the picking. Macy watched the punch right onto his chin until...

ALL. Wham.

JOEY. And he went. Like a falling building, there was brief wobble, and then one side collapsed. He dropped to his left knee, his arm draped over the ropes. More like he was catching his breath than anything. The ref rushed in and started counting, Macy was up at four, the bell went, the round finished, and the whole fight changed.

At the corner. A roar greets SID's *return.*

MICKEY. Good boy!

DREW. Unbelievable.

MICKEY. See how he opened up after that first left? He's been doing it all fight, keep at it.

JOEY. Don't get too confident.

DREW. Yeah, he nearly caught you coming off the ropes.

SID. Didn't though, did he?

DREW. Damn right.

MICKEY. How's that eye looking?

JOEY. Just a bit swollen.

MICKEY. Okay, good lad. Is he looking across at you?

SID *looks over* MICKEY*'s shoulder.*

SID. Yeah.

MICKEY. Good. He's going to come at you now, got it? You embarrassed him and now he's going to try and do the same thing to you.

DREW. Come on, on your feet.

MICKEY. We've got him where we wanted him, all right? Now it's time for you to go to work.

JOEY. Stay off the ropes.

MICKEY. We got a fight on our hands now.

Bell goes, SID *moves into the ring.* JOEY *steps forward.*

JOEY. It's funny watching a fight. See you know your man inside out, from the second he wakes up till when he goes back to sleep you're with him. And then suddenly you're in the fight and you can't do anything. All you get is one minute each round. And you can make little changes, a few suggestions but really you're using that time to stop his nose bleeding and his eyes swelling. You just have to watch as this kid who you've seen grow and change over the years, marches off into the ring, completely alone.

Beat.

He'd had a great start, put down a champion and set the crowd alight, but there's a difference between ready in the gym and seeing it in the ring. When you're fighting someone like Macy they'll always have a little something you didn't expect. And sure enough, by the end of round six Sid was in trouble. Nothing unnerves a boxer like getting hit when he's throwing shots, and Sid was getting beaten to the punch time and again.

SID *flops into the corner.*

MICKEY. Look at the eye, Joe.

DREW. Deep breaths.

MICKEY. Ribs?

DREW. All I can do is ice them.

SID. You said he'd be knackered by now.

DREW. Well, stop making it so easy for him.

MICKEY. Exactly, if he's not feeling it then make him work more, fucking hit him!

SID. I keep getting nailed with the counter.

JOEY. Side to side.

DREW. He's right. You're a sitting bloody target, keep moving.

JOEY. And get at him.

MICKEY. Clearly he's not slowing down like we thought he would so you have got to slow him down. If you are going to get hit each time you go in then stop messing around with little feelers. If you're going to trade punches with him make sure they're punches worth fucking trading, hit him! Put your glove through his bloody head.

JOEY. Up, up, up.

MICKEY. Stop being so polite, take the dancing shoes off and fucking hit him!

DREW *steps forward.*

DREW. It was the defining round of the fight, Sid was behind on the scorecards and we had to do something to change it. So at the beginning of the ninth we sent Sid out telling him to be much more aggressive, to keep moving forward. Sid wasn't that kind of fighter, but if we let him sit back and soak it up we'd all look bad. We had to make a fight of it.

Back to the corner.

MICKEY. That's it, good boy! Get at him.

JOEY. One, two. One, two.

DREW. Easy, careful.

JOEY. Off the ropes, off the ropes!!

Collective groan.

Get your bloody hands up!

MICKEY. Good lad!

DREW. Now with the right!

JOEY. Attaboy!

DREW. Sid's taking a lot of punches, Mick.

MICKEY. Yeah, but he's giving them too. Go on!

JOEY. Good. Get after that eye!

DREW. He can't keep this up for seven more rounds.

MICKEY. It's better than him sitting back and waiting for Macy to take him apart, isn't it? We can't let him have the whole fight his way. You've got to risk stuff, Drew, learn to take risks and hope –

ALL. Oh!

Moment of shock. SID *steps forward.*

SID. I saw them coming. The punches. I saw them. I'd started the round pretty well, taking the fight to Macy just like Mick said. But I'm not a brawler, and I knew I'd slip up eventually. I was pushing Macy back, but I must have thrown one too many because when I saw him winding up to throw the counter I was off-balance. I could see what was coming and knew I had to get out the way but my feet were all wrong and I just had to watch it happen. The jab to my body landed flush just under my heart, stopped me dead. I managed to take some of the sting out of the right cross. But the left uppercut hit me like a train. I felt my legs go and my head snapped back, it's like someone changing the channel, one second I'm watching these shots come in and then suddenly, all I could see were the lights above me.

SID *falls backwards and is caught by the corner.*

JOEY *counts to eight before they hurl him back upright.*

Then he is grabbed and thrown onto the stool.

MICKEY. Water!

JOEY. Is he cut?

DREW. No.

MICKEY. Fucking miracle. You with me, Sid?

Claps about.

DREW. How's your jaw?

SID *has given up.*

SID. I'm done.

DREW. Eh?

MICKEY. He's going to be fine. You've got nine rounds left to steal this, y'hear? Nine more rounds!

SID. I'm done, Mick.

MICKEY. No you're fucking not.

DREW. We could throw in the towel?

JOEY. It was just a bad round, that's all!

MICKEY. He's going to be fine.

SID. I've got nothing left, I'm telling you, Mick, I'm done.

MICKEY. Do you want to quit on your stool? Do you want to be another number on this bastard's record? No! So get back in there and fight. You keep fighting until they ring that final bell!

JOEY. Up, up, up.

MICKEY. Go and get him, Sid!

DREW *steps forward.*

DREW. He didn't even make it through the next round. His legs were shot so he just stood in the middle of the ring and traded punches, bending lower and lower towards the canvas. He got knocked down once more before the ref jumped between them and stopped the fight. The second it was over Macy just turned and headed back to his corner, leaving Sid stumbling around like a pisshead. Job done. It's quite… hard watching someone you care about get treated like that. Outclassed and embarrassed. But he didn't stand a chance, he'd had so much luck getting past all the others that when it finally ran out we saw for the first time how out of his depth he was. Something we should have spotted first.

JOEY *joins* DREW.

JOEY. After the fight we just sat in the changing room. No one spoke, we just sat there, thinking, listening to the stadium empty. When it was all quiet Sid took a shower, and asked Drew to take him home. I figured someone should to talk to the press if we ever wanted a rematch, damage control, so I went out to find reporters. And we left Mickey, sat on his own, just staring at the wall. Zoned out like he'd been the one taking all those punches. So much for bring me that title.

The others drift away, leaving MICKEY *on his own as if in the changing room.*

MICKEY. After that fight I was made. You get someone a title shot, and the world will show up at your front door. The next time I went into work there were five young guys waiting outside my gym, begging me to take them on. No one needed a handshake, no one needed to ask their mum. They'd've sold their teeth to sign with me, which was pretty fortunate as it turned out. One week after the Macy fight I received a letter from the lawyer of a manager named Mark Simmons telling me Mr Sparks has chosen to appoint Mr Simmons as his manager and that my services would no longer be required. That was it, that was all the thanks I got. Turns out Simmons had convinced Sid that it was my fault he lost, my training and my management that let him down, and that if he wanted to win titles he should sign on the dotted line. It was bollocks, Sid lost because he wasn't good enough. At least I got him paid. Simmons got him hurt. But he had a well-known name and a boxer who believed all his promises, easy money. Sid was whisked off as a bit of a novelty, someone for the up-and-comers to cut their teeth on before moving up. He became a journeyman after all, and that title shot never seemed to materialise. He finished with a record of seventy-one fights and forty-three wins. I didn't see him again until just after he retired. I was at York Hall, full house, great atmosphere and one of my boxers had won an earlier fight. They were all celebrating in the changing rooms but I ducked out into the tunnel to see the other bouts. And there he was, standing right next to me, took me a moment to realise who it was he looked so different. Heavier and older, much older than he was, all small eyes and swollen ears decked out in some baggy suit to hide his gut. And he looked like every other boxer you see shuffling around the ring on a fight night, trying to recall their glory days. Because that's the thing about boxers. One day they will come up against someone they can't beat. And it kills them. So we chatted for a bit, I asked what he was going to do now his career was over. I don't think he had a clue. So we just talked about the fights and who was going to win. Then he shuffled off to watch the next generation go at each other. Cyclical, see. We work them, these kids. We grind them and push them and shout at them until one day they can't keep their hands up any more. They start taking punches, and then they don't make any more money. So either they disappear, or they return the favour and go into my line of work. It's not pretty, but we've all got to make a living.

Lights fade to black.

End.

A Nick Hern Book

This revised edition of *Cornermen* first published in Great Britain in 2018 as a paperback original by Nick Hern Books Limited, The Glasshouse, 49a Goldhawk Road, London W12 8QP

First published by Nick Hern Books in *Plays from VAULT* in 2016

Cornermen copyright © 2016, 2018 Oli Forsyth

Oli Forsyth has asserted his moral right to be identified as the author of this work

Cover image by David Lindsay

Designed and typeset by Nick Hern Books, London
Printed in Great Britain by Mimeo Ltd, Huntingdon, Cambridgeshire PE29 6XX

A CIP catalogue record for this book is available from the British Library

ISBN   978 1 84842 742 6

Woodland
CARBON
www.woodlandcarbon.co.uk
NICK HERN BOOKS
Printed on Carbon Captured paper